WHERE THE WAT.

I have known water to be a mysterious thing—full of peace or death, life or danger. In *Where the Water Begins*, Kimberly Casey enters, deliberately and with unquestionable poetic skill, into that uncertainty, that life-giving and taking body. These poems are delicate in their sight and sound, and they hold multitudes of pain, memory, and the way in which the self can always find itself, even in the wash of waves. It is an incredible book, one which takes the reader to her own ocean's bottom and up toward the air which waits above the water's edge. It is a prayer of a book, it is a wrestling which ends in release.
—Ashley M. Jones, author of *REPARATIONS NOW!*

Bearing witness to generational trauma and survival, Kimberly Casey's debut collection asks, "What in our blood begs us to drown ourselves?" With tenderness and honesty, these poems reveal our most human scars—those of the flesh and those of the spirit, the accidental and self-inflicted. When you discover part of yourself reflected in *Where the Water Begins*, honor that wavering image, "[p]raise it for its resilience. Kiss [its] palms."
—Emari DiGiorgio, author of *Girl Torpedo*

In this aptly titled collection, a body of griefs comes to life slowly, slowly, unfurling throughout the pages as quietly as it can, taking the reader by surprise. Here, is a body filled with water, a body filled with scars, a body filled with water-memories, a body filled with deaths it keeps churning and churning upon itself, as if these remembrances will keep the lives lost, and itself, breathing, breathing. There is strength in such brokenness, it seems to say, and the poet does a stunning job of rebuilding it brick by brick, bone by bone, a tender care weaved throughout, as if to say, there is no salvation here, but there is home. And home is riddled with new griefs. Whether the poems are talking about familial relations, or pulling memories out of their graves, or counting the deaths of loved ones, they beckon us with difficult questions; through their tenderness, we are enshrouded with care too, and, suddenly, we find ourselves unspooling too—with this poet, we are reminded that what was once broken, can be mended, slowly, slowly. This is indeed a stunning, stunning collection.

—**Mahtem Shiferraw, author of** *Your Body Is War*

WHERE THE WATER BEGINS

Kimberly Casey

Riot in Your Throat
publishing fierce, feminist poetry

Copyright © Kimberly Casey 2021

No part of this book may be used or performed without written consent from the author, if living, except for critical articles or reviews.

Casey, Kimberly.
1st edition.
ISBN: 978-1-7361386-2-5

Cover Art: Corinna Nicole
Cover Design: Kirsten Birst
Book Design: Shanna Compton
Author Photo: Lauren Gowins

Riot in Your Throat
Arlington, VA
www.riotinyourthroat.com

CONTENTS

11 Another Flood
12 Blame Shift
14 What Lives Between Our Bodies
15 Buzz Cut
17 I Am Asking How Late Is Too Late
19 The Way We Remember
20 Homemade Hot Sauce
22 A Hope or a Prayer
24 Descent from Mt. Shasta
25 The Pressure of Problem Solving
26 Through the Algae Bloom
27 Bottle Cap Collector
29 This, Too, Is a Sacrament
30 Forgotten Function
32 In Her Dining Room
34 Envelop
35 Waves from the Wake
37 Dry
38 An Exercise in Redundancy
40 Woodland Wallpaper
42 Golden Hour
44 Water on Glass
46 The Talk
48 An Open Wound
49 What You Leave With
50 Ode to My Menstrual Cup
52 I'm Not Remembering It Right
53 More Than a Finish Line

54 Grief as Target
56 Service Station
58 A Scar
59 Funeral Cards
60 Keeping Fit
62 Limitless
64 Knocking on Locked Doors
66 Heartbeat
67 Namaste
68 Irish Goodbye
70 Where the Water Begins
72 Decrescendo
74 Undertow
76 Early Garden Life
77 Beauty in Broken Things
79 Instead of Sleeping, I Am Listening

82 Thanks
83 Acknowledgments
84 About the Author
85 About the Press

ANOTHER FLOOD

I sit here, in the knowing but not knowing,
the ghost of a possible tragedy lingering over my shoulder.
In the morning, I steady my breath, return the call.

The chimney stays tightly bound in a tarp.
The buckets on the sunroom floor fill slowly, a drip
like knuckles cracking or the smacking of gum.

He overdosed. He did it in our bathroom.
Joe did everything he could but . . .
I leave work. I drive. I cry. I take Ativan. My heart,
a snapped tree branch. Another love to lay to rest.

The rain won't quit. The Tennessee River floods.
Roads shift and split. The mountains are cracking.
I keep shooting whiskey 'til I can't feel anything.
The lake levels are too high, the dam hard at work
to retain the excess. I drive to the boat ramp

but it's under water. So I sit at the edge, the car idling,
humming a soft hymn. I drive to the waterfall,
so much force falling from the cliff, from the sky,
the rain soaking my hair, the river washing my feet.

I touch the edges of things I know could kill me.
This is how I pray. I stare at the sky and wait
for the clouds to form, telling myself next time
I'll be ready, I'll be able to save him.

BLAME SHIFT

It began with Adam.
The wet car door handle slipped
through my fingers when she told me.
I am already learning to blame
the other woman first. When Mom
moved out, Dad didn't drink
the same way. Apologies ring inside this phone.
Decline. Decline. Decline.

Mom lives somewhere else but keeps
coming home for clothes. I pack
my clothes in my car and move
away from James when he gets locked
up again and cannot chase me.
I allow myself to be seen as object. Living

out of a car is simple when it's just you,
and your dog, and you stay south for the winter.
The south has salvaged my decline too many times.
James' funeral reminds me of the driveway.
I am losing my love for the first time. I am blaming
the wrong person. Mom moves back in
when the lying stops, when the bottles are buried.

Alabama asks me to stay but I'm scared
of the summer. Robert asks me to stay
but I'm scared of being happy.
Summer can't stay forever.

I don't know who to blame. Robert says
I love you and I pick a fight. I am a flower girl,
a bridesmaid. I've kept no dresses.
I am planning a wedding. My dress arrives
and I cannot wear it. I pull petals from flowers
and scatter them around. I get a new mirror.

I wear the dress. I drink. I stop.
I find a new home. I try on new clothes.
I learn to apologize without flinching.
Adam asks me to forgive him
new year's night. Midnight arrives.
I do. I do. I do.

WHAT LIVES BETWEEN OUR BODIES

My dog, curled gently against my hip,
snoring softly. A candle nub still on fire.
The Tennessee River. Someone else's hands.
His liver, blackening. My lungs, blackening.
Mold on the back deck. Water
from the leaking chimney, dripping
into buckets that can never
catch it all. Winter is melting
into our home. Damp coats hang
heavy and my joints ache.
My body, a ventriloquist—put yourself inside me
and my mouth mumbles what you want to hear.
My body, a basin full of flammable liquid,
his anger, a match. My body,
a card given to the grieving,
an offering that is never enough to heal
but opened and read anyway. I kept trying
to break us, just to prove myself right. My body
an unchipped vase, flowers in the hollow.

BUZZ CUT

A mountain of empty cans and cardboard boxes are stacked
against the wall to maintain some suggestion of order.

My credit card is on file at the front desk for the fourth night.
Too many bodies in the bathroom, waiting in line under

the vanity lights next to the coke covered counter, my fingers
collecting nests of hair before they fall to the floor. I am too skinny

for the clothes I've wrapped around myself, hiding my shape
in their folds. I keep repeating 'I love you' to the strangers around me,

imagining his face on their alert, alive bodies, smiling at our ability
to stay awake through all the act changes outside the room—

the pulling of the plug, the removal of the bed, the huddled
family with no reason to stay, unable to leave the last place

he was breathing. After the funeral, we grieve with what killed him,
taunting death. We say *just one more time for his memory and then*

we'll stop. Tomorrow. But if you don't sleep you don't have to wake up
to a world where he is dead. Drunk driving to a drug deal. We've

done it too many times and I was so often in his passenger seat.
This time I wasn't, and the highway sent his body home,

catapulted from the Cadillac into the rain-soaked street.
The passenger, pinned against the median, pushed his way out

to call for help, collapsed. If they were here in this motel room
I would tell the strangers to leave. I would ask the ghosts

to forgive themselves
while washing their hair.

I AM ASKING HOW LATE IS TOO LATE

At 14, I first learn what overdose looks like.

I am 24, holding my breath as I scan the obituaries.

My mother's sleep looks like a funeral.
She lands in Saudi Arabia, patches bodies with duct tape.
She stays camouflaged and keeps her helmet ready.

I am 15 and my mother has returned but remains hidden—
when she speaks I see obituaries between her teeth.

I am 25 and doing yoga every day,
his ring on the front left corner of my mat.

My mother says she hates dreaming of my brother's face
on the bodies of the boys she could not save.

I am 26 and falling in love with another boy I cannot save.

Home from school due to a foot of snow, I drink NyQuil
'til I throw up. I wake up on the bathroom tile,
picking at the grout.

I am 27 and rupturing. The pills make me feel like an ashtray.
I am soft necked, always nodding.

My mother refuses to take pills that could help her sleep.

I am 28 and counting how many hydrocodone it would take.

My mother's car is gone, my father's cup never dry.
When I make myself throw up I call it a forgiveness.

I am 29 and refuse to take the pills that could make me happy,
worrying that they will make me forget him.

She teaches me what an overdose sounds like in your sleep.
the abnormal snoring, a catch in the back of the throat.

I am always adjusting the pillows and checking his pulse.
I am asking how late is too late. I am asking about the smell.
My mother and I are scrapbooking funerals. We are sharing names.

THE WAY WE REMEMBER

The DVD case is gnawed and torn from the teeth
of a dog that is no longer with us, yet every year
my mother pulls it out, puts it on the player,
sinks into the couch. I never understood
who would make a DVD of the 9/11 footage,
who would buy it, sit in their home
and relive the burning bodies falling from windows.
When September returns, her face already wears winter,
frozen and sharp. When the second week rolls around
she's on her side, tucked into the corner of the sectional,
wrapped in a New England Patriots fleece.
On days she has to go on base,
she'll come home in her camos,
prop her boots on the edge of the couch,
grab the same blanket, and stare at the billowing smoke.
She wants to save everyone. My mother's guilt
could survive anything, live with the cockroaches,
make them keep a clean house. Her photos
from Iraq are on a disc, pictures of the bodies
she could not fix. The first year after,
she asked me to watch the footage with her.
I couldn't sit still. The next year I avoided
the living room, kept my head down
on my way into the kitchen.

HOMEMADE HOT SAUCE

The pepper plants keep producing after the first freeze of the year,
branches stiff with ice, weighted with ripe cayenne and habanero.
Even though I haven't showered, stuck wearing the same stained
black hoodie with torn thumbholes in the sleeves, I cook
hot sauce, red pepper jelly, salsa, stir-fries—anything to eat
the abundance in the bottom of the crisper drawer.
Every morning I pick more, too many to keep up with,
but I can't bring myself to uproot the plants.
I pack Ziploc bags and gift them to friends.
I try to make jalapeño poppers.

I envy the plants, alive and well, vibrant
orange and red despite the turning weather.
I don't want to unwrap myself from the gray blanket
but eventually I pull myself from the bed,
shove my feet into worn slippers,
take my medication, move to the kitchen.

> *1. Deseed and roughly chop 12 peppers. Sauté with minced garlic, salt, and olive oil on low heat until softened.*

> The pan scrapes against the eye of the stove as I occasionally stir.

> *2. Add 1 cup vinegar and bring to a boil. Add orange slices, mango, or other fruit if desired for flavor.*

> The sour scent spreads and my eyes start to water.

3. *Boil for 15–20 minutes, until the peppers soften and begin to break down.*

    I wash my hands but do not wipe my eyes.

4. *Let the mixture cool.*

    I swipe my phone with sticky fingers, but I don't know who to call.

5. *Transfer to a blender or food processor. Blend on high until the mixture is as thin as you prefer.*

    I dump the tangy concoction into the blender, and the softened pulpy peppers spin and split.

6. *Taste. Add more peppers if additional heat is desired.*

    I play old voicemails. I keep myself alive.

A HOPE OR A PRAYER

I cannot write about God   without writing about violence.
Madeline is five weeks old,   in the emergency room.
My brother hasn't slept,   hovering over her bed.

We take Ativan   across time zones.
Facetime freezes us   across state lines.
I want to be there.   I am 1,172 miles away.

My uncle got a new liver two weeks ago.
We hadn't spoken in years, but I would still give
a piece of my liver, but his body was too broken.

He needed to take it all.
Some young boy died so he could keep killing himself.
My father says God has a plan for all of us.

I text my brother pictures of my dog making silly faces.
We laugh so our bodies can feel something.
I hope he can get some sleep.

I hope they can give her   everything she needs to live.
Madeline can't breathe.   They give her more oxygen.
She is on a ventilator.   They give her more antibiotics.

Hope is a rainstorm.   Prayer is an umbrella.
I lost prayer long ago,   but hope stays
curved at the edges,   an anchor.

Madeline can breathe again,	and so can we.
My brother can sleep again,	but it's lighter.

My palms press together out of habit.
I pray to my family. I pray for their strength
to continue. They are the pillars I believe in.

DESCENT FROM MT. SHASTA

Precious ecosystem
of organs, peculiar
in its acidity and
cellular species,
some extinct,
some seeking growth
by voyaging to new viscera.

I study this community—
frail plants, invasive insects,
misshapen stones of amethyst,
tissue and cysts, a deep brown
blood loosely clotting—

strain green tea leaves
through the teeth,
drinking a dirty river. Pluck
an apple, scarred red sinew.
My body is a homeland
I've often tried to leave behind.

Cross-legged on a mountaintop
after walking a rock labyrinth
to an altar of items left for ghosts,
a dragonfly lands on the peninsula
of my knee, resting then flying away.
I am reminded how easy it could be
to disappear without violence.

THE PRESSURE OF PROBLEM SOLVING

Amy Winehouse was booed off the stage for being too tipsy to perform
a month before she died of alcohol poisoning, and those same fans
mourned, whispering *I wish she had just asked for help*.

And I was there somewhere, singing along to "Stronger Than Me"
dipping my pinky into plastic bags, fishing for motivation
to make it through the night. 27 seemed a far-off age.

She howled through "Rehab" bellowing her dissent,
her voice through speakers declaring broken
being better than sober. I only play guitar

when I've been drinking. My steps stumble
but my fingers flow. I used to sing
but sobriety felt like I had nothing
valuable to put to a medley.

I am trying to untangle creativity from healing.
I don't want to burden art with expectations,
I want to fix myself so I can write poems

that don't remind addicts of what they're missing.
How do I undo eighteen years of writing
tied to the pressure of solving problems?

I write about the happy people I see on the street,
the way the mulberry tree in the backyard blooms.
And I realize that I am there somewhere,
among the beautiful things. A part of this landscape.

THROUGH THE ALGAE BLOOM
She thinks fishing is an odd way to make love.
—"Perfume River" by Mary Ruefle

The only sounds are the flick and swish
of the rod sending bait into the water
and the slick flip of each page turn.

He drops the trolling motor,
it rumbles softly beneath the water
pulling us through the algae bloom.
He takes his foot off the pedal,
pulls the motor back up, lets us coast.

The baby herons squawk
while nested safely in the pine,
know their voices will carry
far enough to call their mother home.

Striped bass are jumping
making rippling targets he can cast to.
He says every fish smells different,
sniffing toward the mouth, smiling,
removing the hook, gently
dropping the fish back into the water.

There are so many ways to make love.
The trust of new wings.
Our satisfying quiet.
The boat kissing the water.
The chase. The catch.
The fish letting go, accepting.
The release.

BOTTLE CAP COLLECTOR

There are so many almosts my mouth has swallowed
that holding my tongue becomes my native language.

The warped wood of the deck is still swollen
with the weeks of rain, but I lie

flat on my back and let the sun beat my bones,
pull off my shirt, nest it under my heavy head

letting my spine sink between the slats
and stare at the bare trees above

waiting for the exact moment that death becomes bloom,
and I wonder if my own body holds the same power.

I still miss the man that walked with me
the last time depression burrowed into me this deep.

I wonder what could have been if I was more prepared,
if I had been going to therapy before we met, was medicated.

I imagine an alternate reality where I asked for his keys
just minutes sooner. This is the first day of sun

where I don't feel like I don't deserve it.
Where I don't feel so responsible for his death.

I still wonder why I called that night for the first time in months,
and why it happened to be just an hour too late.

I memorize the surface of this blame,
a tongue interrogating a wounded cheek.

I pick up every stray bottle cap I can find
and work the worry of my thumb into them

hoping to send a signal to its missing body.

THIS, TOO, IS A SACRAMENT
This is how you make
your world small enough for you
to wake up each morning and breathe.
—"Creed" by Kwame Dawes

Run before the sun comes up, before the humidity drags your lungs to the pavement. Once you catch your breath, head to the backyard garden and touch each plant, inspect for new life, admire the way the vines find new directions for growth. Keep them from crowding and smothering each other. Sling the satchel across your back. Pick blueberries, dropping them into the bag producing a simple staccato percussion. Rather than taking one at a time, let your fingers curl around the bunches and pull. Forgive yourself for the ripe ones you let slip to the earth. The birds and the squirrels will clean up your messes and you have enough harvest to fill a freezer. When you sit down to sip your coffee, read the news. Put a bowl of fresh berries next to your left hand. Every time you read of a new death put a new berry into your mouth. Notice how full you become. Notice how life can be pulped between your own white teeth. And even though you haven't eaten red meat in 11 years that doesn't mean you didn't inherit incisors. Leave the juice dripping from your lips. When you put on your mask and go to the protest, remember the stains you've made that others can't see. Remember that pulling out your own teeth won't undo the damage of the past.

FORGOTTEN FUNCTION

The tired VCR wheezed & whirred to life,
my fingerprints pressed into the dust on the top.
A reminder of what we can't throw away.

It was the fourth day home from work
post-op. Twelve more days to go.
I'd already watched all the DVDs
and the lack of internet I once found
charming and freeing, now infuriating.

I'd forgotten how to connect the thing.
Uncoiled tough black cords and searched
for an input. Settled it on the shelf
and swiped my sleeve across the front,
my Fall Risk band tucked beneath.

I carry the old dust with me back
to the couch as the VCR rewinds.
Before I can press play, I settle
the heating pad on my stomach
the ice pack against my back,
blanket over my bruised body.

The VCR knows how to play
after all this time. Still holds
the tape safe within itself,
the two spools working in tandem.
Catching, releasing, present
becoming past.

My left ovary, growing
and releasing cysts. My right,
releasing nothing at all.
Blood sheds back into my body
and tissue adheres to the wrong organs.

There are scars inside me.
A forgotten function.
A question of relevancy
and womanhood. I fall
asleep to an old movie,
wake to the bright blue screen,
the blinking zeros, the reset.

IN HER DINING ROOM

The back porch is full of beer.
My uncles bring bottles in their pockets.
The cousins sneak vodka into soda cans
and try to stifle giggles in the basement.
My grandmother forgets her wineglass
in the dining room and fills a new one.
No one has a problem because we're all
doing it together.

Working at a diner at fourteen years old
trained my grandmother to nourish
her nine children—set the table, serve plates,
keep everyone full. She left home at sixteen
after meeting my grandfather—served him
scrambled eggs and he fell for her.

At her funeral, my uncles wander to the car
to crack into cans of shared memories.
On the ride home they get pulled over,
the trunk open, empties rolling into the street.
They say their mother just died
and the cop lets them go.

I show up still drunk from last night,
do shots of whiskey, stumble to the bar
with cousins and uncles, January wind
tears the warmth from our bones.
My grandfather sits silent by the fire

working his way through a thirty-pack.
No one has a problem
because we are all grieving together.

My aunt is in rehab. My uncle drinks O'Doul's.
Their siblings tease them at the dinner table
over a messy sandwich tray and deviled eggs,
saying it isn't alcoholism, it's just social drinking,
telling them to lighten up while tossing them a beer.
Crabs in a bucket, pulling each other back in.

ENVELOP

I like making my own dark.
As a child I'd crawl into the hall closet,
listening to the muffled sounds of my family in motion
imagining them as strangers.
It is a controllable night. I knew I could step out
into the smell of cinnamon rolls and baseball blaring on AM radio.
I still seek out small containers—
an aimless car ride with the music too loud.
Under the bed with the aging cat cradled in my arms.
Tucked into a sleeping bag in a child sized tent.
Wrapped up in his hoodie, with all my limbs tucked inside.
A camper in the country, bundled in blankets under a skylight,
able to see the vast wonder around me without touching it,
just sitting in awe, feeling small but held, sheltered
within a make-believe safety. I fear the violent whisper
of wind creaking through a shut window.
He was buried in the smallest box. Six feet
of skin and muscle I memorized with my fingertips,
gone. I used to sleep wrapped in the weight of his limbs.
Now he is underground, and I sleep furled like a fiddlehead,
harvested before the frond reached its full height.
I close my eyes but specks of ash still stir into my sight.

WAVES FROM THE WAKE

If you forget something, does it linger
in your 5th vertebra, a smoothed pebble
causing you to pause, ask yourself how it got there, or

is it called forgetting if you do it on purpose—
With life jackets stripped off and folded into pillows,
limbs tossed over each other, staring at the sky,

we rock with the waves from the wake
of a slow passing pontoon without speaking.

I want to forget the funerals
but I don't want to forget the people we buried.
Today we try to let go of the losses.

Our fishing poles are pointed toward the water
but the lines aren't let out yet, no bait set—
the hooks wait to snag the muscles of a mouth.

We lay like this until the mosquitoes start
sniffing for sweet blood,
before we start killing them
with chemicals, with our hands,
leaving a graveyard
glistening on the surface of the water.

Sleepy and sunburnt we return to shore,
my cell phone buzzing

and the car radio
counting the number of people lost.

The world has always been dying,
we've been losing people every day,
it's all we can look at.

But we have this lake.
We can row away from the ramp
unafraid of the water.

WOODLAND WALLPAPER

The bunk bed was braced against
yellowed, peeling wallpaper
an eternal autumn, leaves piled
around the picture of a fawn.

Four generations of fingerprints
have patterned the perked ears,
carved down the curve of the neck,
slept dreaming of a familiar forest.

Grandfather's computer glowing
bright blue creates a cage
around the empty bed frame.
Do not touch the dark,

the crumbling plaster.
The fawn doesn't live
on that wall anymore.
Your grandfather,

paper bleached and creased
unglued and folding in on himself.
The fawn forgot the forest.
Your mother

ripped away the walls while
"Blue Spirit Blues" billowed up the stairs.

to make into totems. The three silver dice
stored in the side pocket. His lighter
with a peeling skeleton on the side.
The pocketknife with the red handle and dull blade.

So I just keep naming them, a mantra organizing
everything in the room, in the world,
trying to keep observing, trying to remember
what I can still touch.

AN EXERCISE IN REDUNDANCY

Every day I look in the mirror,
a Post-it sticks to the chest of my reflection,
my therapist's personal phone number
to use if the day ever comes
where I decide to stop.

Every day I stare at my feet and try to run
at the same pace, but I always rush through the familiar.
The 1.23-mile loop, an exercise in redundancy,
passing the same houses, same loose dogs,
same kids on bicycles with oversized helmets.

Every day my dog rests curled against my hip
heating the whole world under the blanket,
snoring like a motorboat flooding underwater.
She wakes and licks my face relentlessly,
and I wonder how much time passes by while she sleeps.

Every day I grab the backpack with patches
from the states it has traveled stitched
onto each pocket and swatch of fleshy fabric,
shoulder shift the weight and go to work,
grateful for a job.

My therapist recommends naming five things
within reach to come back from a panic attack.
I always struggle with the fifth, afraid
of excluding items I've saturated with memory

DRY

The dishwasher is full & there are more
in the sink & the grass itches my calves
& the birds are eating the unpicked mulberries
now fallen to waste & patching this roof
has taken 6 months & even the succulents
are too dry & you keep your prayers
a secret & you let them go
like lightning bugs & they flutter flash fade
from your hands & I've never felt
so thrown away & all the same I ask
about your day & all the same your voice
overlaps mine & you tell me I'm young enough
to get better & you say you're too old & too broken
& there are footprints you won't erase & you
won't share your own mother's story & I'm forgetting
her name & all I remember is the open field
where I'd practice running
away & the broken open beehives
dried out by the sun.

scraps piled in the middle,
the room a fire in waiting,
a precisely picked scab.

GOLDEN HOUR

When you caught one to keep,
we took it home and I asked you to teach me.
You showed me how to spike the brain—
I thanked the fish, looked away, pressed down.
We bled it, shaved away the scales,
severed meat from bone.

I'm afraid of leaving my loved ones alone.
Flying into an endless sunset the next day,
a soft glow through the window,
and every passenger is glazed
a smooth bronze. Every other seat empty,
each face masked, some with simple fabric, others
medical-grade filtration set beneath serious eyes.

No one here talks much.
Bodies pull away from the aisle
each time a passenger scurries by.
If a plane crashes in the middle of a pandemic,
would the world make a sound?
How do we grieve
one loss among so many?

Yesterday the breeze caught the water
making waves beneath the boat,
and you swayed staring out
towards the setting sun.
Your skin slick with sweat

bronzed in the light bouncing
under the bridge where you waited
for something to bite—

I told you I didn't understand
the need to maim something
just to send it swimming back below
with a taste of blood.
You said we are all violent.
It's about finding the way out
that does the least damage.

WATER ON GLASS

His body blocked the doorway, bulky in a red winter coat.
The basement echoed with his yelling,
but the loud music upstairs hid it from our friends.

I urged him to hand our puppy over to me—
I curled the wriggling dog to my chest
while watching him pace in front of the doorframe.

I don't remember why he was mad,
I just remember counting the items around me:
the open toolbox, the paint cans, the bottle of Jack.

I wanted to go back to the party but my body
stuck to the cement floor, knowing what would happen
if I tried. I worried if I left now,

it would be the last time I saw him alive.
He stomped off into the snow, screaming
I knew you never gave a shit about me,

once I'm gone, you'll be sorry.
I laid on the cool basement floor until
someone scooped me up in their arms,

asked if he hit me.
I said no, even with the blood
working its way to my collar.

When the phone rang at 6 AM
I knew before I answered.
Now, on the days when I call his mother

like I promised I would,
I speak kindly of him, avoid talk
of baggies and blackouts. When his sister calls me,

we talk about the apple pies we made together,
the beef brisket slow-cooked all day, smoke trailing down the driveway,
how he ate like a garbage disposal, noises and all, and we laugh

like those moments didn't lead into nights
where we would get calls from him, on a new street,
on a new drug, screaming that shadows were coming for him.

I try to revive him in my mind
but instead all I can see is water on glass
as bits of his life bead up and roll away.

THE TALK

Maya tells me she had to have the talk
with her twelve-year-old last week—
I wonder aloud what prompted her,
a girlfriend, or something he said.
She corrects me.

*Not that talk Kimberly. The talk where I tell him
how to act around police. To never go into a store with a hood up.
To keep his hands out of his pockets. To never turn, never run.*

I think back to the Boston jewelry store I worked at in college.
The boss ordered us to follow around every group of black kids
to make sure they weren't stealing. Once he accused some teenagers.
When they tried to leave, he tackled them down the stairs.
They didn't have anything. The police called it an honest mistake.

There are brown bodies in the street bleeding out.
Maya tells her son to not watch the videos,
but he's already seen them. She tells him
black boys should be full of joy, not full of holes,
that his smile is a revolution. When I apologize,
she shakes her head. *It's just something we live with.*

There are nine hoodies hanging in my closet. My hands
fold into their pockets most fall days. I remember
my aunt holding tight to her purse when
we passed a black man on the way to the playground.
I've crossed the street when the sidewalk

seemed too full of people who didn't look like me.
I didn't quit that job at the jewelry store.
I never said anything to the boss. I did what I was told,
followed kids around the store and cashed my paycheck.

AN OPEN WOUND

I punched a hole through the closet door. It fell away flimsy under my fist and I didn't find the healing that I'd hoped for. I wanted to stop being angry, put all that emotion somewhere, but was left with just a broken door. My husband put a poster over the new absence, but I still know it's there when I turn towards it each evening. It's instinct to break something in solidarity with myself. My father once punched a hole in the bathroom door, through the plaster in the stairwell too. I don't think he felt better after. There is a sense of control in creating an open wound, knowing we can fix it later. I am not violent with anyone but myself anymore. I once took a swing at him for saying I was too drunk to drive. I hurt him for stopping me from hurting myself. I thought the pain was a part of my personality. I admit I once wanted to not get better. There is a pride in being damaged, a sick too easy to get stuck in. When the notary stamped the final page, allowing us to part from the past, it felt like plaster breaking. It felt like something flimsy finally giving out. I loved that sound of leaving. It reminded me of the mesh and spackle sanded down, softened edges, just like new.

WHAT YOU LEAVE WITH

The mixing bowl speckled with water stains from the dripping ceiling. The frayed phone charger wrapped with Band-Aids in lieu of tape. Two torn towels. The tightly bound sleeping bag and tent. A suitcase full of books. The bruised rim of an eye socket. An alarm clock that runs too fast. The neon life preserver with the compass attached. A serving table turned writing desk. A handmade stained-glass lamp. A full-length mirror. Your mother's teapot. Your father's bookshelf. The softest blanket you can find. Two tool kits. Mismatched curtains. Running shoes. A cast iron skillet. A coffee pot. An umbrella.

ODE TO MY MENSTRUAL CUP

At first, I feared fishing it out,
fingers touching blood clots,
but releasing the mess
satisfied something in me.
No longer caught in cotton,
the pieces of me were free
to float away. I remember
the pain of others,
but now I nearly forget I'm bleeding
until I'm ready.

I shower and unseal myself safely
watch the red splatter
expand then collect
down the drain.
When the week is done
I boil the cup—
buoyant silicone chalice
bouncing around a bubbling cauldron,
the witchcraft of making something dirty
become clean again.

I want to sip whiskey from this sturdy shot glass,
or use it as a serving spoon, let it be seen
it all its wonder. Behold the flexible flower
forever bloomed. Behold the keeper
of quiet waste, tiny basin for my body.
Praise it for its resilience

during 12-hour work shifts
without a private bathroom.
Praise it for letting me sleep in
without worrying about the sheets.

Praise it for its gentle way of keeping me
in touch with my agitated body,
breasts swollen, skin inflamed.
This ritual of filling and emptying
reminding me I am still here, alive,
reminding me to let the bad blood go.

I'M NOT REMEMBERING IT RIGHT

When someone you love stumbles into a pyramid scheme,
if you have the means you buy the product and let it gather dust.

My aunt pressed her hand to my forehead to sense
my energy, pulling her fingers, prescribing four different bottles,

and my parents pulled out their wallets. I can still remember
the feeling of the vial dripping clear liquid numbing under my tongue,

the feeling of six pills sliding slowly down my throat, learning
to dry swallow when I was too tired to trek downstairs.

The smell: wet grass and mulch.
The texture: dry, speckled butter beans.

My mother tells me I'm not remembering it right;
she never made me take strange supplements.

After dinner I excuse myself to the bathroom and open the closet.
The childhood clutter is gone. No stacks of vitamins, no herbs to see.

No half empty bottles, proof to help iron the furrow from her brow.
Just his inhaler, cough drops, allergy pills, Band-Aids, dust.

MORE THAN A FINISH LINE

The boat pitches to the side and rocks
as blurred bodies on jet skis rush past either side,
one hollering as he pulls ahead of his friend,
rounds a distant buoy. We move away, become
more than a finish line.

My mother once told me to imagine
holding a bubble in each hand while playing piano
to keep my hands curved, keep my wrists
from dragging down.

This new house holds so many bubbles—
the right side of the bed, the TV stand,
the half empty bookcase, cabinets scattered
with mismatched dishes.

Floating face up in the deep blue lake
ears rocking in and out of the water,
a relentlessly bright sky, eyes shut tight,
I hear him ask if I'm made of air.

I image a bubble inside, keeping everything
from collapsing in on itself.

GRIEF AS TARGET

The tumor took
over half her jaw.
He points to the X-ray
circling the dark spot
with the cap of his pen.
Her head looks barely
bigger than a walnut.
I try to find something
to compare the tumor to,
but it stays a tumor. It grew
so quickly. She wasn't in pain
long, just a few days of drool
and no appetite, a bit of blood
on the chin. When she goes,
she is sedated, so
it's hard to know the moment.

They light a candle. I don't cry.
I've learned the danger of vulnerability
in front of men I do not know.
I stopped crying at funerals when
I lost a love and someone hugged me
a little too long, a little too tight.
A grieving woman is still a target.
If she does not cry, she is cold,
if she does, she needs consoling.
I grieve quietly, in private.
Maybe I hold on to things too long.

I reach for ways to bind my wounds
faster. At my grandmother's funeral,
it became a joke among my uncles
of who would cry first. My mom
gave a eulogy while they shed tears,
her own never falling. We tell each other
it's better this way, it was time.
Later, I heard her through a closed door.

My husband on misty-eyed drive,
I clean up the litter box, the cat food,
the crate. There is always more
to do. In the shower I make lists,
think about the day ahead, anything
to keep me from falling apart,
becoming the water around me.

SERVICE STATION

The Honda Civic had a busted air conditioner
since the day I bought it two years before.
I followed I-40 through the Southern states,
pressing through as many hours as I could.
With no money for hotels, I kept a tent
in the trunk and found state parks to settle in,
or napped in the back seat at a rest stop
while gripping my knife next to my belly.

August in New Mexico, I kept my windows down
with a sweatshirt on my arm covering sunburn.
I hadn't seen a gas station for about two hours.
No sunscreen. Tank almost empty.
I pulled off at the next exit to find pumps
where the numbers still spun on dials.

Twenty minutes go by before
a tall, disheveled man takes his post
behind the counter, never taking his eyes off me
while ringing up my water and gas.
He didn't say anything.

I stared at the yellowed tile floor,
hurried back to my car, caught my reflection
in the green paint of the driver's door,
bags bulging under my eyes,
hair on top of my head in a loose bun,
t-shirt torn at the shoulders.

I looked so small,
a woman alone on a road trip
in the middle of the country,
halfway between where I'd been
and where I wanted to be.
Windows open, inviting in the air,
but with it comes the dirt.

A SCAR

O, to live on the furling purple
planet on your calf, that blooming bruise,
live a lifetime in three days before
the world fades away and the last thing I feel
is the throbbing of your blood. O, to make a home
on the scars on your arms, in its valleys and sloping hillsides.
The accident, a totaled motorcycle, clothes
clipped away to save your life. If I lived there,
I would thank your skin for scabbing over
and healing to create such a monument,
I'd take morning treks to climb
up mounds of muscle,
build a bonfire in a nearby freckle.

FUNERAL CARDS

I count the names of the lost boys
like a mantra, beads thumping together
as I thumb through each,
their cause of death like a last name.

Keegan suicide. Joe car crash.
James overdose. Quinton suicide.
Andrew overdose. Danny suicide.
Evan overdose. Alex suicide.
Sean overdose.

A stacked deck of funeral cards
sits in my desk drawer,
separated into suit—psalm,
song lyrics, poem, tribute.

I only visit when I add new names,
an afterlife built of altars.
Corners faded and worn, I can't fit them all.
I worry I forget a name and they'll disappear forever.
I bury grief in my body before we bury them in the earth.

KEEPING FIT

The gym has "no man's land"
painted over the door to the women's-only workout room.
I keep my hood up until I'm inside.

Each machine in the room
with peeling leather and cracked paint. Each woman in the room
with eyes low, headphones on.

I started going to the gym
when I started drinking again to keep a balance inside my body.
I still feel guilty.

I run until I can no longer feel my legs.
Until I cannot see through my matted hair. Until
I don't feel like yesterday.

I curl weights up
toward my chin. My arms ache and my heels dig into the ground.
There is a strength in stubbornness.

My phone still chimes
with alerts from work, from my emails, from my husband. I try
to type while on the bike,

hoping I can sweat
some meaning out of my skin. Write a draft of a poem I'll never revise.
Some things don't get finished,

the trick is to not let them
keep you up at night. We're going back to the brewery later
where I'll talk about the gym,

fishing for something
to settle my shame. My skin is breaking out. My eyes always irritated.
I am working on the wrong muscles.

I am always tired
but never sleeping. I am always exercising but never strong enough
to recover what that night took from me.

I blame my body
for all the wrong things. I take responsibility in the wrong direction.
I want to control something.

Before I fall asleep, I set my alarm.
I stretch my arms up above my head, stand on my toes,
feeling the tearing of muscle.

The neighbor's porch light
peeks into my bedroom window. The space heater glows red,
clicking as coils struggle to heat the night.

LIMITLESS

Joe asked if I wanted to go fast. I nodded,
putting down my beer, grabbing the heavy helmet.
Dozens of motorcycles lined up for the memorial ride,
so many strangers stood around the coolers sharing stories.
We all thought we knew him so well, but if that were true,
we'd have met before this.

My chest pressed to Joe's spine,
hands locked around opposite wrists,
hugging close to get more speed.
My cheek pressed against soft padding,
the helmet's visor whistling at its seams.

After the official ride's route was complete
we hit Rt. 20—two lanes straight across an expanse of nothing
connecting our tiny towns through a tunnel of trees.
When we hit 100 mph, I smiled, 115 and my eyes narrowed,
129 and I finally closed them, imagining what would happen
if I let go, let my body become a lost kite.

But I stayed,
opened my eyes to top out at 132, then the numbers
began rolling backwards until we stopped to wait for the others.
Joe asked how it felt and my mouth still hadn't caught up yet.
I wanted to say I could forget that two people I had loved
with this body had died in the last two months
and on that bike it felt possible to drive away from it all.
Instead, I just said *limitless*.

8 years and 1500 miles later their ghosts still catch up with me
tugging my hair, gnawing my nails, asking why
I quit visiting, asking if I think I'm better
than them for getting out of town, slowing down.

I try to stay sober, try not to cut
and when the urge to join them returns
I still imagine my body lifted in the air
like a kite, but now I have a tether.

I don't I want to leave anymore, even though
I still imagine leaving, even though
I still blackout and drive home hoping to die
the same way they did, tragic accidents,
rain pulling our tires toward the edge.

KNOCKING ON LOCKED DOORS

I would like to unlock that door,
turn the rusty key
and hold each fallen one in my arms
but I cannot, I cannot.
I can only sit here on earth
at my place at the table.
—"Locked Doors" by Anne Sexton

Inside the closet in the spare room
inside the trunk buried under clothes to donate
inside the shoebox for heels I no longer have
is where I keep the people I've lost.

Leafing through the letters I find three keys,
two silver, one brass, inside an envelope.
It has been five years since they touched
the keyholes they belong to,

but I haven't thrown them away.
I test them on every locked door
hoping to find a room I once knew.

In dreams, my teeth are keys
and everything I bite into opens
memories of ghosts. A slice of toast
and Joe is in the kitchen, beer and biscuits
for breakfast after partying all night.

I gnaw on a piece of gristle
and James' mother is serving us Thanksgiving brisket
before he got too high to want to eat anymore.

Baked macaroni and my grandmother arrives,
clears plates from the table, asks if I want to play cards,
passes me a cup of tea.

When the food is gone,
my teeth fall out and the keys
sear broken lifelines into my palms.

HEARTBEAT

When I discovered it would be easier for me
to develop cysts and scars than get pregnant

I asked the doctor to take away the damage.
I knew I wouldn't need a uterus or ovaries anyway.

She said I was too young, too unwed, to be certain.
I've never wanted to bring children into this world.

If I did get pregnant, it is likely I'd miscarry
and be persecuted for the potential life lost.

I claim my hometown as a defense mechanism
every time Alabama makes the national news.

My mother calls me, says I can always move back home.
I tell her if everyone in their right mind leaves the south

what happens to the kids who aren't old enough to leave
or the people without the means to move.

I remind my mother that the misogyny of men
reaches across state lines, reaches deep into our history.

My father doesn't talk about it. His God
hears every heartbeat and calls it life.

NAMASTE

Even here you hold tight to time,
always worried about wasting it,
but I don't blame you. Just know
that the longer we balance our bodies here
the stronger our muscles will grow,
the more of each other we can come to know,
the rush of vein, tug of tendon.

If you stand sturdy, I will bend beautifully.
If you lift me, I will calm your shoulders,
my palms pressing into the arc of your arm.
If you keep lookout, I will close my eyes
and whisper what our future will bring.
I see our daughter's heart in your chest—
soft and curious, beating fearlessly.

This family bruises so beautifully
because all our blood
comes to surface together.
We share it all in some way.

Precarious maybe, but strong enough
to feel it and still make our own light.
There is bravery here.
I am asking you to hold me
in the exact way
I need to be held.

IRISH GOODBYE

Green beer tilts towards the rim of my plastic cup
as I dig in my bag to find my phone.
Rising from the picnic table bench,
I answer my mother's call, trying to find
a quiet corner of the bar, but it's St. Patrick's Day.
Cheers and chattering fade as I cross the parking lot.

I stick to the tar when she tells me,
Your Uncle is in the hospital
on the transplant list for a new liver.
He's denying doing the damage
to himself. I've had two Irish car bombs,
two stouts, one green ale.

She'll text me with updates.
I stumble back to the table.
Someone tells me they love me
and I can't look at their face.
I am the family I come from.

I let a few tears tumble to the dark wood
after I order another shot and beer,
though I am already not sitting straight.
I bum cigarettes, flicking a lighter in my left hand,
sparking and fading.

I would give him a piece of my own organ
if I could, if we matched, even though
we stopped speaking three years ago.

He once told me if his house was on fire
he wouldn't want a woman firefighter to come,
since she would be too weak to save him.

I wonder if he feels that a woman's liver
would be too weak for his broken, bloated body.
Since we stopped speaking,
his house did burn down.
I never got to ask who saved him.

My anger weaves itself around my ribs,
catching everything I wish I could say.
I stand up to smoke, settle on the edge
of the table to tell stories of his lake house,
drinking vodka out of soda cans on the boat
as he opened another bottle of wine,
the sun barely past its peak.

It's easy to act like we're different people
until I order another beer and black out.
What in our blood begs us to drown ourselves?

Someone kisses me on the cheek
as I dangle my feet off the edge of the table,
imagining the days on the end of the dock,
dragging our toes through the ink-stain lake.
I pick at a splinter in my palm,
prodding the pain. I don't remember leaving.
I don't think I said goodbye,
just stumbled down the sidewalk to the next bar.

WHERE THE WATER BEGINS

The lake thins, tunnels through thick forest.
We chase the creek, navigating over fell trees
until the water clears. We hop out into the sand
and pull the boat gently toward the base of a rock face
where the cold current disappears into a cave.
Rain runoff drips slow from the fractures in the stone,
nature's metronome. Fish flee beneath pond moss.
He stands still enough to split in two.

Here, no one else exists, just us and our doubles.
Mirrored bodies connected at the ankles
slowly reeling in the lure, quiet casting, repeat.
There is a particular trust in letting someone see
your split self—the version of you that only arrives
when the world stills and sharpens.

I count the folds in the rock face,
my own mirrored self, holding a half-eaten apple
staring at the upside-down sky.
I hope when this Saturday strains through the sieve of age
I am left with enough mud to make a statue

to honor every bit, even the stuck boat
scraping against bloated bark and branches,
the hopeful firewood wedged into the V of a tree
refusing to split, the pile of bear shit on the beach
we have to hop over to get to the water,
the jawbone of a deer left by the coyotes
and washed down the rocks to decay and bleach.

The sun settles behind the tree line
so we build a fire, simmer the coals to cook,
and make a plan to hike to the top of the cliff
and search for the rest of the deer's skull
before starting the motor, stirring the water,
sending ripples to erase our reflections.

DECRESCENDO

The keyboard finally retired
as our lease expired.
Decades sitting side stage
covered in glitter and sequins,
now no one knew who to return it to.

After the last late night,
running beer-soaked bags to the dumpster,
mopping, bleaching bathrooms,
I slipped out of sight
behind the curtain and took it home,
swept the debris from each key
as it hum-popped into life.

My fingers curved to position
as they had at my grandmother's piano,
my feet barely able to reach the pedals,
playing Silent Night in July
as Nana sipped wine,
rocking in her recliner.

Mom's hulking 1980s Yamaha
used to live under her bed.
I'd sit cross-legged on the floor,
leafing through her torn sheet music—
The Beatles, or Holiday Classics,
stretching to create chord.

Her fingers could move
from an afternoon of playing shortstop
and float over the keys.
I used to push on the veins
of the back of her hand
or twist her wedding ring
up to her knuckle.

Now I sit at this stolen piano.
My hands rise up from the wrists,
my own veins beginning to bulge
from an afternoon in the garden,
pulling weeds from the raised beds
and clipping kale leaves,
knuckles swollen, playing
sleep in heavenly peace.

UNDERTOW

A mop-headed boy screams at a seagull who swooped down,
plucking up his bag of Flamin' Hot Cheetos. He swipes
at the falling puffs, scooping what he can salvage
from the sand, stuffing his mouth before his sister says no.

A man uses his hands to dig into the sand, sculpting a seat
for his love to nest into next to him, their sunhats' thin brims
fluttering in the breeze. They sleep in the heat
holding hands, heads drooping toward each other.

I am steps away from an ocean I escaped eight years ago.
I hesitate to go in, for fear of that familiar sting of salt.
My husband and I are steps away from separating, though
we still call each other daily, end with *I love yous.*

I do not say this aloud to the friends beside me. I want
to trap the secret a bit longer, until I learn the new language.
I inch toward the water alone. I let my feet become swallowed.
My calves tense as they submerge, my body becoming buoy.

I brace my belly against an unexpected wave.
Or perhaps I did see it coming all along,
felt this swell inside instinctually.
I sharply inhale and go under.

There is no one else—
no more screaming boy or reprimanding sister,
no longtime lovers entangled in the sand,
no more scavenging seagulls or teens tossing a football,

no broad bed to lie lonely in. A wave shifts me from this silence
and I emerge again, walk to the spot where my friends sleep
under scarves and sunglasses, toes turned toward the sky.

When I return, they won't hear the shells cracking
under my feet. They will offer chocolate and wine,
build a billowing fire in the stone pit,
tell me I am not to blame. I am not broken.

I did not break anything. For now, I let them rest
as the tide shifts, and the surf slips further away.

EARLY GARDEN LIFE

After 22 days of Alabama rain
there's finally one day of sun.
I break apart pallets to build
raised bed gardens. The boards
pop away from the frame
and are piled near the fence line.
After building three beds
and spreading dirt to dry out,
I start to clean up the wood scraps
and spot a salamander
just like the ones in Massachusetts
I used search for under heavy boulders.
Slick belly always dragging the dirt
but staying so clean. I wonder
about the lungs, the brittle of bone,
and feel a familiar urge to pick it up
in cupped hands, rub my thumb
down the ridge of spine, carry it home,
confine it in a plastic case
next to half empty coffee cups and
books I swear I'll get back to.
But I resist. Instead,
I admire the shimmer of skin
in sunlight. Remove the wood
from around the salamander
leaving some planks behind
and watch it slip out of sight.

BEAUTY IN BROKEN THINGS

The mouth wants us to remember the names
of the soft things we used to pray to. It craves
becoming an altar, hosting the notes of totems behind teeth.

I feel like I am only my mouth these days,
reciting exit strategies and crisis management
while forgetting the body propelling me.

Today I nourish my mouth, plump mulberries
fresh plucked, ripe cherry tomatoes,
the biting bitter of a halved grapefruit.

Murmur mantras into a mirror.
Stop smoking for the second time.
Stop drinking, again. I'm tired

of feeding myself only broken things.
I want to stop repeating the wounds,
and instead, remember beauty.

Witness the good among the garbage.
Recycled art exhibiting all around me
if I could only stop to see it.

Kiss my love's temple. Try to smile
towards the sun like the newly planted peppers
reaching for their light.

Take my medication without guilt.
Stop gnawing on fingernails. Floss.
Sing. Laugh. Yawn.

Rub balm onto my chapped pink lips
and quit biting at the broken. Let my tongue
float to the floor of my unclenched jaw.

Praise it for its resilience. Kiss my palms.
Holy is the healing we do
for no one but ourselves.

INSTEAD OF SLEEPING, I AM LISTENING

Bubbles break brightly against aluminum
in the seltzer water can on the bedside table
next to the alarm clock set two hours too fast
and the taser found at work. Nights
turn shadows into hulking men with hollow eyes
and this sound, a simple sprinkle of rain inside a can
passes time, counting the minutes until
it goes flat, and sobering silence is all that remains.
8 full days from the last sip of alcohol—
sleep is starting to become less erratic,
but every sound becomes amplified.
The neighbors van differs from the Hummer,
one with squeaking breaks, the other
with an angry engine. Sometimes they leave
along with the sun, other times, hours apart
in the middle of the night. The dog has stopped
growling under her breath, regardless of the time.
She kicks her back legs, chasing them in a dream.
The ceiling fan needs to be balanced—
the chain clangs against the light fixture
no matter the speed. The TV light is too bright
and talk radio makes one too aware
of all the ways the world is dying.
I turn over, tuck my palm below my ear
and am left alone with that hollow song
of my own determined heart.

THANKS

I am endlessly grateful for my family, especially my parents, who continue to push me to become the best version of myself while loving me unconditionally every step of the way.

Many thanks to my Pacific University cohort including Zac Furlough, Ana Michalowski, Sarah Elkins, Melissa McKinstry, and Therese Carr for the phone calls, emails, writing prompts, impromptu poetry readings, and for keeping me moving forward on this project and in life. Thank you to poet inspirations Shira Erlichman, Ashley M. Jones, and Emari Digiorgio. Thank you to Courtney LeBlanc and Riot in Your Throat press for believing in my work.

I am forever indebted to the friends who supported me through all the grief within these poems, and helped me heal. Thank you to Robert Daniel, Maya Cotton, Sara Bowen, Bob & Addie Gile, Lauren Gowins, Nick Hudson, Spencer Cochran, Matt Broadhurst, and Denise Duffey. Thank you to everyone at Out Loud Huntsville for the encouragement, vulnerability and inspiration, as well as my Patreon supporters for believing in this project before it existed, including Cash Daugard, Matt & Ari Pepper, and Josh Dickson. To the whole 5 town crew for making me who I am. To Sean Martin, James Fraser, and Joe Felton—I love and miss you every day.

These pages wouldn't exist without the support and direction from my advisors at the Pacific University MFA program, Kwame Dawes, Ellen Bass, Mahtem Shiferraw, and Dorianne Laux, along with workshop leaders Joe Millar, Shara McCallum, and Marvin Bell. I am in awe of their talents, their guidance, and their generosity.

ACKNOWLEDGMENTS

Gratitude and appreciation to the following journals in which these poems first appeared, sometimes in earlier versions or with different titles:

Ink & Nebula: "I Am Asking How Late Is Too Late"
Lost Balloon Magazine: "This, Too, Is a Sacrament"
Passengers Journal: "What Lives Between Our Bodies"
POETRY: "Golden Hour" and "Irish Goodbye"
Simple Machines: "Limitless" and "Blame Shift"
Soren Lit: Homemade Hot Sauce, Bottlecap Collector
SWWIM: "Grief as Target"
The Giving Room Review: "Forgotten Function", "Dry", and "Knocking on Locked Doors"

ABOUT THE AUTHOR

Kimberly Casey was born and raised in Massachusetts, though she now calls Huntsville, Alabama home. She is the Founder and President of Out Loud Huntsville, a nonprofit organization dedicated to inspiring community outreach and activism through written and spoken word. She received her MFA from Pacific University in 2021. Kimberly was a member and coach of the Out Loud HSV Slam Team from 2017–2019. Kimberly has competed at Southern Fried, CUPSI, Texas Grand Slam, and performed at venues across the country. She hosts and organizes a wide array of literary events such as youth poet meet-ups, storytelling events, workshops on craft, performance workshops, and more. She is the Editor for the *Out Loud HSV: A Year in Review* anthology. Find more information on the author at kimberlycpoetry.com.

ABOUT THE PRESS

Riot in Your Throat is an independent press
that publishes fierce, feminist poetry.

Support independent authors, artists, and presses.

Visit us online:
www.riotinyourthroat.com

CPSIA information can be obtained
at www.ICGtesting.com
Printed in the USA
BVHW032333150821
614145BV00002B/91

9 781736 138625